Collecting

Stamps

A Beginner's Guide to Basics of Discovering,
Recognizing and Collecting Stamps So You Can
Build Your Collection as a Hobby or as an Income
Source

By Jerry Haydock

Contents

Thank you for buying this book and I hope that you will find it useful. If you will want to share your thoughts on this book, you can do so by leaving a review on the Amazon page, it helps me out a lot.

Introduction

The interesting thing about albums. Initially, they keep memories-- maintain remembrances of your child's 11th birthday celebration someplace in a hectic restaurant in downtown Rio de Janeiro, the volleyball competition on the beach that one summertime day, the photo of a well-known painting in the museum which you got reprimanded for, security personnel warning to kick you out.

That's most likely the initial album you take out of the dirty shelves to show to buddies-- to ensure that you could tell them how a policeman in Paris gave you that stern, cautioning glance and all you might come up with was "oui, monsieur, je m' excuse.".

Next, this entire thing regarding albums might have brought about a fad referred to as scrapbooking. An offshoot probably, however, who knows for how long it is going to be around.

Suddenly there are online sites promoting the pastime of scrapbooking. Your neighborhood stores are offering all things pertaining to scrapbooking.

But collecting stamps and albums? Now, that's a classic. It has actually stayed à la mode, even if it began ages back, 140 years to be precise. Collectors of stamps have their own customized albums.

And as experienced and expert philatelists are going to claim, "simply ensure you have ample pages in your album to have plenty of stamps." Some individuals have actually been known to have more stamp albums than picture albums within their attic.

Stamp collecting is a "mature" pastime-- not due to the fact that its satisfaction is confined to older grownups-- the shut-ins as we like to name them-- who obtain much satisfaction from looking at the trees and the flowers, the towers, the planes, the fish in the sea; not just in their area yet in locations as remote as American Samoa and Papua New Guinea.

Stamp collecting is a mature pastime due to its part in history, due to how it has actually developed into a hobby that has brought delight to countless individuals all over the globe.

It's a pastime that incites something in every collector-- a yearning to go to foreign lands, an eager investigative feeling for color and print errors, a yearning for relationships, and an intellectual interest about what others are up to or have actually found.

Photos in an album maintain those Kodak times that could not be relived once again. They set off friendly and funny discussions amongst aunts and cousins and great grandfathers, and they remind individuals of what it was like when their hair was curly ten years back and not dyed.

However, stamps in an album? How about history, culture and geography to start? How about relationships that recognize no frontiers or barriers? How about an intense enthusiasm that never lessens or flickers?

This is the charm of collecting stamps. It opens doors, it's the limitless well of wisdom, and it's the story in pictures of a nation and its heritage. It's additionally about the story of the people who work 5 days a week to bring our mail. It has to do with stamp dealers who deal and wheel and understand everything about price and value and rarity. It is or was, at one time, about me and you.

This book is going to take you on a trip of the delights of collecting stamps as a pastime, the terms and signs utilized by stamp collectors, the tools you'll require should you come to be a collector one day, and how to begin. There's additionally a part in this book about the resources you can use to make your pastime as satisfying and pleasant as you desire it to be.

Chapter 1: Stamp Collecting Joys

You are going to most likely meet very few individuals who claim they have actually never collected anything in their life. However, there are individuals who, even when not intentionally collecting a specific item, have a tendency to have more than one of the certain item. It could be anything-- tennis socks of various colors, books by a specific author, CDs of their favorite vocalist or brand name trainers.

And after that, there are individuals who intentionally collect-- foreign-made lighters, baseball cards, crystal vases from Europe, classic coffee mugs or crochet hooks from the Far East. And there's an explanation for their collection.

One may claim, "oh, I was in this baseball game viewing it idly. When I turned around, I noticed Mark McGwire-- he had a baseball cap on and a smile. I thought he was the prettiest thing in the arena, so I wound up collecting anything that pertained to baseball.".

Why do individuals collect stamps? The reasons do not differ from those mentioned by baseball card collectors. It specifies our characters, it's a type of individual entertainment and satisfaction, it's a chance to find out more about stamps and the nations that provide them. It supplies an chance for like-minded collectors to develop relationships and exchange knowledge.

There are added delights when it comes to stamp collecting: it is an excellent way to glance into a nation's history, geography, science and biography, and sports. A stamp, specifically when it is wonderfully created in an appealing mix of colors, stimulates human curiosity.

Initially, the images and colors draw in individuals, and after that, they look deeper at the stamp to see what it means. For example, if somebody from the Czech Republic notices a Canadian stamp with a maple leaf or a beaver, the individual getting the letter may be lured to learn more about the maple tree and/or the beavers.

Stamp collecting additionally pleases our wish for order, proportion, and organization. Some individuals might begin their stamp collecting by placing stamps into a shoebox. However, there is going to come a time when those pieces are going to have to be arranged. By collecting stamps, our organizational abilities end up being carefully developed. And the visual benefits could be mentally pleasing.

Collecting stamps opens our eyes to travelling, and while we are unable to take a trip to each nation in the world in our lifetime, our stamp collection is going to reveal to us sites and lands that we have actually not yet explored and present us to a nation's fauna and flora, of high powered hydroelectric dams, of mountains and cliffs that no person has actually attempted to venture out to. Anybody who begins to collect stamps can continue at his own rate and at his own impulse. However, collecting stamps-- or the field of philately-- is a disciplined field.

There are requirements and guidelines that direct the philately study, and there is a significant quantity of literature that records the knowledge from longtime collectors of stamps. Research continues, and there is constantly brand-new knowledge to be acquired.

Nobody needs to pay very much for supporting a pastime like stamp collecting. Actually, a pricey collection does not always suggest that it's the most intriguing or the most important.

Rather, it is the manner in which the collector has actually arranged his collection in an intriguing way due to his experience and knowledge. Lots of prize-winning collections which have actually been declared "impressive" in club programs typically began as affordable undertakings.

While a couple of stamps collectors have a financial investment goal in mind, the appeal of stamp collecting lies in the pure satisfaction of the pastime. Think just how much more there is to be gained if you simply kicked back and huddled on your couch to appreciate your collection. If you see your collection as a monetary investment, then you'll want to acquaint yourself with assessing the worth of your collection, finding out about stamp auctions, and discovering the ideal dealers.

Generating income out of one's collection is an option, however, consider the many other opportunities available to you if you didn't restrict yourself to profit intent.

Stamp collecting is approximately 140 years old. Everything began when England released its initial stamp on May 6, 1840. There's an amusing story about one of the earliest attempts at collecting stamps. A lady put an advertisement in a British paper trying to find all types of secondhand stamps so she might wallpaper her room.

The actual fun began, nevertheless, when post offices understood that stamp collecting could be a substantial source of profits. Given the production of various stamps in a given year, individuals branched off to "motif" collecting, rather than restricting themselves to "nation" collecting. A couple of collectors have actually even started collecting stamps to tell a story or concentrate on a famous person's bio. However, this would require a whole lot of research.

The pleasures of stamp collecting are enhanced due to the fact that it is not a pricey pastime. In the first couple of months, collectors do not need to invest a penny, other than asking for secondhand stamps from family and friends and fellow office workers.

Individuals who were once collectors and who quit the pastime would be happy to give away their collections with the hope that it could be continued by the individual taking control of it.

They have actually felt the pleasures of collecting stamps one time, so they would be just too excited to assist a starting collector.

Stamp collectors are going to additionally discover a lot of assistance from neighborhood stamp clubs, their neighborhood post office, and the Web. Stamp collecting is an extensive topic in the online world, and the novice is going to be pleased to find how many resources are accessible to him.

Chapter 2: Terminology

Perforations

The initial stamps that came out were without perforations, however, cutting them ended up being troublesome. Perforating machines entered into usage to resolve this issue. They punch holes horizontally and vertically so that stamps could be separated from the sheet more quickly.

Even after stamps started getting perforations, post offices additionally generated stamps that were not perforated to assist collectors in collecting them. A perforated stamp has "perf" attributes, and the perfs go by number. Certain stamps have perf # 11 on one side and perhaps a perf # 9 vertically.

So perforations can be found in various sizes. The bigger the holes, the less perfs there are on the stamp side.

Postmarks

Have you ever got in a competition where one of the guidelines specifies that all entries "have to be postmarked no later than the last day of the year?" When post offices have the letters and other things sent by mail by the public, they are going to mark the stamps as "canceled." This is to demonstrate that the stamp has actually been utilized so that individuals do not utilize them once again. Post offices, in some cases, utilized a type of hammer damp with ink to strike the stamp.

Envelopes/ First Day Covers

When collectors conserve the envelopes with stamps on them, it is referred to as first day cover collecting or just "covers" for brief. This is an intriguing part of stamp collecting since the covers really offer information about a specific significant event.

3 parts enter into a first-day cover: stamp, envelope and postmark.The last element-- postmark-- is the crucial element as it indicates the date on which a specific stamp was canceled. Normally, the U.S. Postal Service launches a stamp in one city on the day prior to the beginning of a sale of a brand-new issue.

A brand-new stamp that is released is typically a reason for celebration.

Commemoratives

Commemoratives are stamps which highlight or "celebrate" an individual or occasion. For instance, the initial moon landing by American astronauts resulted in a commemorative stamp to call attention to this turning point. While the stamp might be lovely, the first-day cover is more significant due to the fact that it includes information about the occasion.

Additional intriguing commemorative was the crowning of Queen Elizabeth. In Canada, the first-day cover was released by the name of "Coronation" in Alberta!

Overprints and Perfins

As we will through all the terms, are you in some way getting the sensation that there are numerous aspects to collecting stamps that you could concentrate on? When stamps actually have something composed on them, there is generally a meaning there.

For instance, the tutorial site of the British Philatelic Society stated that the letters "OHMS" might be placed "over the stamp," which indicates (on His Majesty's Service).

Punching of the letters into the stamp leaves little holes, and they are referred to as "perfins." The word "Perfins" represents PERforated INitialS. This was to prevent postal workers from looting stamps for their own usage.

For collecting functions, for that reason, you might consider collecting only perfins that show the names of the business. This is one collecting field which might fascinate you at a later time.

Coil Stamps

Coil stamps can be found in long rolls and they don't have perforations on bottom and top sides. Due to the fact that they are linked to stamps in the strip, they don't have to be perforated on the other edges. Keep in mind that coil stamps might be horizontal or vertical coil.

Booklet Pane

Stamps were once offered in "booklets." The booklets normally had a sheet of 5 or 6 stamps. Every one of these sheets was referred to as a pane.

Errors

Stamp collectors invest hours trying to find errors. It appears that making fun of individuals' errors is a preferred human leisure activity. The identical theory applies to collecting stamps. Collectors have a good time when they do find an error.

And due to the fact that errors are not a thing you see daily thanks to automated stamp production, when errors do happen, the stamps could be worth a lot.

For example, the United States and Canada have stamps that have the middle part inverted.

While certain errors are not going to fetch you a substantial quantity of cash in stamp clubs or auctions, they are still fascinating to the majority of collectors. An excellent source of collecting fun would be the Canadian "Admirals" issues of 1911-1925.

They are not truly errors, however, they do have small distinctions. Color errors are additionally frequent. When a color is overlooked in the printing, this is seen as an error. So the following time you purchase stamps, check them out more carefully.

Perforations might additionally include errors. Lots of stamps have perfs going right through the center. Collecting stamps does not end with the fundamental terms. As you end up being more advanced in the activity, you might be inspired to start going to stamp dealerships and stamp programs.

You are going to be coming across some symbols-- generally a symbol like an "asterisk" or acronym (2 to 3 letters) that are utilized by stamp dealerships.

Unused and used stamps have symbols: "*" for unused, "0" for used, and "**" for unused.

These symbols do not have any secrets to them. When a stamp is put out of commission (post office places a mark on the stamp), then it is seen as used. If the stamp is still active, then the stamp is unused.

Have you ever licked the opposite stamp side so you could attach it to your envelope and after that send it? Did licking it ever leave a pleasurable or uncomfortable taste in your mouth? Believe it or not, gum plays a big role in evaluating the worth of a stamp. A stamp's gum condition could be identified by the next letters:

NH

Never hinged: this suggests the stamp has never ever had a hinge on it. NH can additionally indicate that the gum needs to be in such a condition where there are no marks of any sort.

H

Hinged: the gum has actually had a hinge put on it.

LH

Lightly hinged: the mark is little or small a hinge put on the gun.

HH

Heavily hinged: the mark is extremely noticeable after the gum has actually been hinged.

HR

Hinge Remnant: a part of the hinge put on the gum was hard to get rid of that it was left in location, connected to the stamp.

DG

Disturbed gum: the gum was damaged in some other way. Fingerprints, bubbling or glazing could add to this damage. The gum has actually been harmed somehow, aside from hinging.

NG

No gum: there is no gum, the stamp is not used
Numerous other symbols are utilized; however,
the above-mentioned are the more typically
utilized. Additionally, you might experience the
word "centering" which is another factor in a
stamp's worth.

Chapter 3: Necessary Tools and Supplies

Thankfully, collecting stamps is not as costly a hockey or snowboarding, where the materials and tools needed cost countless dollars. Ski or hockey clothing are really costly.

Collecting stamps is what we 'd call an "economically comfy" pastime. Unless you sign up with the big boys and look at it as a financial investment, practicing the pastime should not cost too much.

Eventually, as you advance in your journey of collecting stamps, you'll need to take your stamps out of that old shoebox beneath your bed so you could install them on a stamp album. Similarly to a picture album, stamp albums are a way of keeping your stamps securely and arranging them in whichever way you desire.

A high-quality stamp album should have a lot of area for an expanding collection, and have a sturdy binding which will not separate the album sheets quickly. Every page needs to be adequately dense with acid-free paper.

Albums for stamps are specialized, and you are going to discover a wide range of albums being offered by retailers. Due to their experience and discussions with collectors, makers comprehend the crucial functions of an album. Some instances of stamp albums consist of:

Minuteman Album.

An excellent novice's album particularly produced US stamp collectors.

Scott's Basic Album.

Album for Canadian stamp collectos.

Scott National Album (Loose Leaf).

This is the market standard for US stamp expert collectors.

H.E. Harris Statesman Album Kit.

This is a perfect starter package for stamps collectors from all across the globe.

Stamp Catalogs

Stamp catalogs are vital tools. Catalogs are exceptional references for understanding the present worth of stamps, and they supply information on how to recognize them and collect them effectively. If you're not ready to purchase a stamp catalog, your public library holds them. Certain catalogs can be found in about 5 or 6 albums.

Watermark Detector

If you wish to analyze the printed pattern embossed on the stamp, you could utilize a watermark detector. Not every stamp has a watermark; however, similar stamps, for instance, might have distinct watermarks.

Watermarks can assist in discovering forgeries and can help in recognizing stamp varieties.

Stamp Tongs

In case you manage stamps with your fingers, you might be leaving fingerprints on them, hence reducing their value. To prevent this, you are going to utilize stamp tongs (tweezer-like tools which are utilized for managing stamps.

In case your collection has actually been recognized as a high value one, the final thing you wish to do is NOT utilize tongs! Collectors might pick from either plastic or stainless-steel tongs. They're approximately 3 to 5 inches long; excellent sets could be acquired for $5.00 to $15.00, however, there are high-end designs that sell for substantially more.

Stamp collectors who are professionals additionally utilize an extremely distinct tong with really pointed tips so that just a tiny part of the stamp is touched.

Magnifier

Lots of stamps are so small you can not even find the letters on them. And if your vision is not precisely that of a hawk, a magnifier ought to fix this issue.

A magnifier is going to allow you to see particulars that you may otherwise not have actually seen or simply to assist you in analyzing its qualities, along with its conditions.

Color Guides

Stamps have some of the more lovely colors ever made. There are publications, properly named Color Guides that can help collectors in determining the numerous colors utilized by stamp producers all over the world.

Perforation Gauge

As we discussed previously, perforations vary in type and size. A perforation gauge assists collectors to split stamps on a sheet and assists in determining which stamp is which. While stamps might look similar, they might have a distinct perforation.

Glassine Envelopes

Prior to placing stamps on an album, you want to keep them someplace safe. This is the function that glassine envelopes have. They are transparent, slim envelopes and can be found in different sizes.

Prior to being prepared for being placed in albums, stamps have to be arranged by style or by nation, and these envelopes are perfect for that job. You can additionally utilize glassine envelopes to send stamps to a buddy or a relative.

Fluids for Lifting Stamps

When somebody sends you stamps still on envelopes, you could get rid of the stamps by utilizing stamp-lifting fluids. These compounds are utilized to "lift" stamps off from different kinds of paper without harming them. They are utilized when utilizing water is not going to get the job done.

Hinges/Safe Vinyl Installs

When you're prepared to mount your precious stamps on an album, you are going to require hinges or safe vinyl stamp mounts. These hinges are offered currently pre-folded to simplify things for the collecor.

The tinier section is dampened, and after that, pushed into the middle of the stamp, upper part, after which the bigger section is additionally dampened, and after that, the stamp is mounted. Care should be taken in dampening as the gum on a mint stamp might stay with the album page too, hence making it tough to get rid of the stamp later on.

Stamp Publications

Turning your collection into a smart collection needs literature you can use. Thus, stamp newsletters and periodicals and publications are going to open doors for you if you wish to broaden into another stamp collecting field.

It's not only about revealing your collection to buddies with pride, it's about having the ability to speak about a part of your collection in an extremely enlightening and informative way. Reading about the current advancements in philately is going to make you value the pastime at a greater level.

Chapter 4: Beginning Your Pastime.

Certainly, the primary step is to obtain stamps. Lots of starting collectors barely pay for anything when they're simply beginning to construct a collection. Speak to your family and friends and coworkers in the workplace and tell them you wish to have their stamps in case they do not desire them.

Word of mouth is powerful. Very soon, you're getting stamps from individuals you have not even met. Sign up with a collector club. It does not need to be a high-brow, fancy club if you're simply beginning. Initially, find out the essentials, and when you're prepared to specialize, then sign up with a bigger club -one that's a regional chapter, rather than simply a community-based organization.

By signing up with clubs, you get to expand your collection since fellow collectors are going to offer you their duplicates. When you have actually set aside ample cash, you could purchase stamps as many collectors do.

This consists of trying to find a dealer; make certain the dealer has an excellent credibility and is licensed to take part in the trade. They normally put advertisements in papers and publications, and are going to join a trade show in your city or town. You could write to dealerships to inquire if they would send you stamps on approval. They send you a set, you keep what you desire and send back the rest.

When you have actually begun collecting, you are going to want to choose what theme(s) you are going to utilize to develop your collection. Or you might want to focus on collecting just mint stamps (the ones that were never canceled) or on canceled stamps. Lots of collectors choose the latter, as it costs less.

In purchasing stamps, start with mixes. These are stamps that are unsorted and that some dealerships are going to offer based upon weight. You have a tendency to stumble upon duplicates when you purchase mixes. This should not worry you. You merely exchange them for stamps you do not have at your following club conference.

Desire even more? Purchase packets. Packets do not include any duplicates, however, they are more costly. Otherwise, collectors are going to go with stamp set. A set typically has all government-issued stamps; sets could be either broken or whole. A broken set indicates that one or more stamps aren't there.

Got all your stamps? The next action is to arrange them. You additionally want to separate them from their backings. Pick which ones you are going to work initially. Place the remainder in glassine envelopes up until you're prepared to tackle them. Do not attempt to rip them since the threat of harming them is substantial.

Attempt immersing them in warmish water in a tidy dish and allow them to soak up until they split from the paper or envelope. Use blotters to blot them dry, or utilize a face towel. If your stamps wind up old and wrinkly, place them in between paper sheets and place a paperweight on them overnight.

If you pick to do nation collecting, organize them in stacks and do it in alphabetical order by the nation. When you have actually completed arranging them, you can begin placing them in your album.

Prior to mounting them, nevertheless, sort them once more -- and this time based upon the stamp condition. Place the best stamps in the album.

Do not establish a psychological connection to all your stamps, the way investors stay with their stocks. Not all stamps, however, deserve keeping. Just condition of the stamp and its rarity are going to identify its worth.

Stamp Grades

Wish to know how collectors and dealers grade stamps? Here's a summary:

Superb

This suggests the stamp is like new with a fresh and tidy color. No tears or creases mark the stamp. It is completely centered with equal margins on each side. The perforation is flawless and total.

Very Fine

A physically flawless stamp-- like a model of sorts. Color may be somewhat off, and margins are a little unequal. It does not equate to a superb stamp.

Fine

A stamp which is devoid of problems or spots or flaws, however, it is not up the superb or very fine requirements.

Good

This stamp doesn't have wrinkles or tears. Color might be toned down, or it might be greatly postmarked. It might additionally be a little off-center.

Poor

Extremely low-grade stamps. They might have a tear or might be creased. They may even have thin areas. Hang on to them just if they can't be replaced.

Now it's time to open your album to mount your stamps. Make certain you have your magnifier, catalogs and tongs prepared. Bear in mind that high quality albums are going to supply a lot of space for you to manage your stamps easily.

Each location for a stamp is additionally plainly marked. In certain albums, pictures of the stamps are printed so all you have to do is place the stamp across the image.

Among the initial steps in stamp collecting is purchasing your stamps. Follow these ideas when you invest in obtaining your stamp supply; you ought to particularly beware when you plan to purchase uncommon or really costly stamps.

Check out the dealer or seller. Was he advised by another collector? Is his name on the list of licensed dealers? It is appropriate to presume that a dealer who has actually been offering stamps for a very long time is reputable and is, for that reason, okay to deal with. He ought to additionally belong to a philatelic society or the American Stamp Dealers' Association.

Recognize the stamp properly. When you head to a dealer, make certain his collection is correctly identified in regards to paper, color, perforations, watermarks, and so on.

These functions contribute to figuring out the market worth of stamps. Stamp catalogs are great references to use when recognizing stamps.

Evaluate the stamp's condition. Utilize the criteria supplied previously in this book. Look for creases, tears, perforations, marks. Stamps in bad condition are not worth the cash, regardless of how low the price is.

Figure out whether the stamp is being sold at a reasonable price. You may do this by looking at the Scott Standard Postage Stamp Catalog. Keep in mind, nevertheless, that catalog prices are just estimations, as many stamps sell beneath their brochure values.

Attempt to establish an eager sense of spotting forgeries or fakes. To the typical collector, it might be a little difficult to tell a real stamp from a repaired one.

Unless you think your stamp collection is extremely costly, it might not be worth the cash to utilize the specialist evaluator services which some philatelic companies charge.

Extra Tips!

2 more ideas for you: Have you got stained or dirty stamps in your collection? Attempt soaking them thoroughly in a tiny amount of pure fluid dishwashing cleaning agent (not dishwasher detergent-- there is a distinction!), then rinse the stamps in cool, clean water.

In case your stamps are terribly stained, attempt cleaning them in a mild water solution and a little bit of enzyme laundry detergent, however, be really, really cautious. This may prove too effective and get rid of the printing ink also.

A note regarding stamps that are self-adhesive. These were generated in the United States at the beginning of the 90s. These stamps you could soak in water, however, you can't do the identical for self-adhesive stamps created at an earlier time.

Certain self-adhesive stamps are created with an unique, water-soluble backing, and even though you could soak them, they simply take longer, like an hour or two. If you do not wish to soak them, simply slice the paper as close as you can, making certain you do not touch the perforations, and after that, place them on your album.

Chapter 5: Resources for Collecting Stamps

Stamp collecting is an improving pastime since it has informative and cultural worth. In about 6 months, you will have found out about nations and special occasions, and a great deal about the stamp collecting market too. You are going to most likely meet a great deal of fascinating fellow stamp collectors with whom you could swap news and notes.

Stamp collectors, nevertheless, need to attempt to get knowledge continually by reading and by signing up with clubs and workshops and speaking with as many dealers as feasible so that they get a taste of existing market news. We'll begin with the fundamental references you are going to want to assist you in getting a much better comprehension of stamp collecting:

Books

Here are some tips for collectors of stamps:

About Stamps: An Illustrated Encyclopedia of Philatelic Terms

This was composed by Wayne L. Youngblood, and it aims both the newbie and the more advanced collectors. The reference is abundant in top quality photos and supplies references.

It speaks about Omnibus issues, Cinderella stamps and utilizes terms as socked-on-the-nose cancel. In paperback format, released in 2000 by Krause Publications.

The World Encyclopedia of Stamps & Stamp Collecting: The Ultimate Illustrated Reference to Over 3000 of the World's Best Stamps, and a Professional Guide ... and Perfecting a Spectacular Collection (Hardcover)

As the title indicates, this gorgeous hardcover is the guide to the finest stamps the world has to offer.

The Romance of Stamp Collecting: Notes From the World of Stamps, Stamp Collecting and Stamp Collectors

This book by Ernest Anthony Kehr is costly, given that it was released by T Krowell Company in 1947! However, collectors of stamps who are enthusiastic about their pastime ar are going to be brought in by the title-- who couldn't use a little bit of love even during collecting stamps? Stamp collectors additionally share their experiences.

Blackbook Price Guide to United States Postage Stamps

This INCREDIBLY great book is a total price listing and reference of United States stamps as far back as 1847! It's effectively arranged (by means of the Scott numbering system), and additionally has some terrific ideas on taking care of, and grading, stamps.

Stamp Collecting

By Stephen Datz, This enjoyable, simple to read, and introductory book about collecting stamps is a necessity for brand-new stamp collectors. It covers where to discover stamps, grading stamps, and how to construct a collection from the initial stamp to the thousandth. It additionally has a fantastic glossary for terms that have to do with collecting stamps.

All About Stamps: An Illustrated Encyclopedia of Philatelic Terms

This enormously beneficial book from Wayne Youngblood is an appeal all its own. It includes photos of stamps, reference information, and insight into all there is to understand about collecting stamps. A necessity for the brand-new and considerable collector as well!

Postal Service Guide to U.S. Stamps

This terrific resource, released by the USPS, takes readers on a lovely historical trip of United States stamps and collecting stamps. It consists of each stamp ever issued by the USPS, and has stunning illustrations which are guaranteed to impress each collector, beginner and professional alike!

Stamp Collecting for Dummies

What book list suggestions would be complete without an acknowledgment of the remarkably prominent Dummies series? Stamp Collecting for Dummies is a terrific and simple intro to the pastime. It deals with how to obtain stamps, how to maintain them arranged, how to take care of them, and how to make money with them.

CONCLUSION

Stamp collecting is most likely among man's older pursuits that could be identified as "wholesome" and "appealing.".

It is wholesome due to the cultural and academic worth that collectors are treated to each time they obtain a stamp.

Once they get one, then they test their knowledge when they attempt to determine which stamp they are dealing with. Whether one is a grandchild or a grandfather, stamp collecting can provide numerous hours of satisfaction.

It's on you to choose whether you wish to pursue a pricey pastime or one that is within your spending plan, for collecting stamps could be both.

While it holds true that there are numerous stamps all across the globe which are out of grasp of the typical collector, there are many thousands-- out of the 200,000 acknowledged ranges-- that are just going to cost a couple of cents to have.

As evidence that stamp collecting is a pastime with a big following, there are supposedly around 30 million collectors of stamps all across the globe, and 10 million of them remain in Canada and the Us.

While numerous stamp collectors are delighted, there are those who take part in the pastime out of isolation. Stamps have actually been known to boost the spirits of downtrodden spirits, and when they find an error, their spirits skyrocket-- for who can withstand telling anybody that they discovered a mistake.

These errors could be a source of laughter and delight. Maybe post offices intentionally produce one or two in each issue due to the fact that they know that unfortunate individuals end up being delighted-- even if just for a short while-- when they discover a slip-up.

Many individuals who reside on the fast lane are going to most likely wish to slow down eventually in their lives, consumed by what in contemporary society is known as a "burnout." Burnout is such a trendy term nowadays, merely due to the fact that it can tear entire beings apart. Obviously, there's Yoga, or your parish priest, or that unopened Sangria bottle, imported directly from the Andalucia.

However, maybe stamp collecting could be the long-term remedy to being hurried and rushed. It can most likely decelerate the aging as well, because as soon as you are hooked, you are going to go more and more after the stamps and diving into the secrets of their message. With stamp collecting, we could be kids once again, thrilled with each discovery since we simply found a real mint among the lot.

I hope that you enjoyed reading through this book and that you have found it useful. If you want to share your thoughts on this book, you can do so by leaving a review on the Amazon page. Have a great rest of the day.

Printed in Great Britain
by Amazon